DEERS
4-Kids

Save the Planet Series

Author Artist   Jeri Lee C.Ht.

Copyright Jerilee.com
2022

ISBN: 9798361325382

Sample
Color

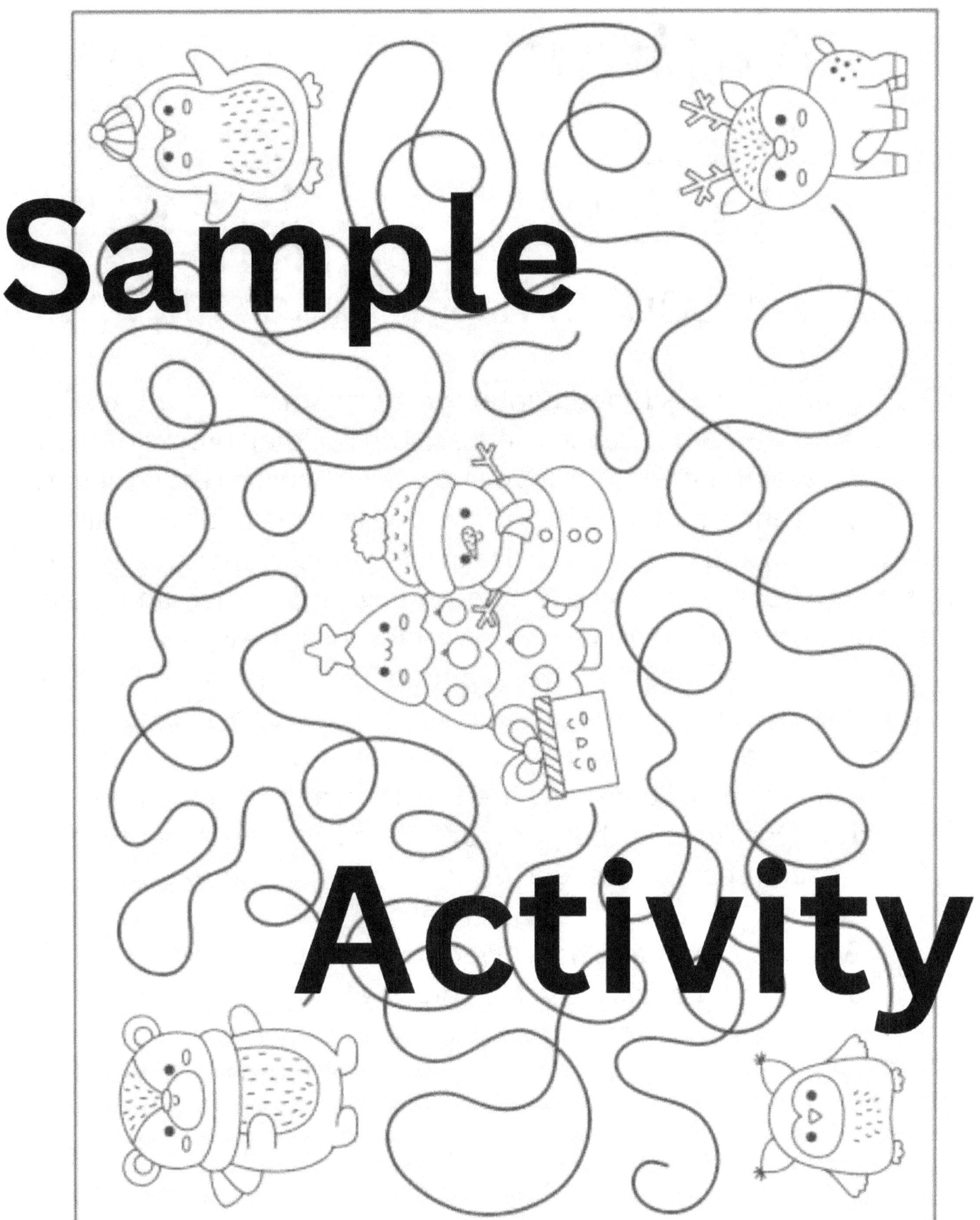
Sample
Activity

Author
and
Artist
Jeri LeeC.Ht.

Early education is fundamental for the children in our life. The ABCs and 1-2-3s we teach them are the building blocks of their future. We first give them love and care. Then we teach them to walk and talk and right from wrong. Next is their formal education and how to socialize in their environment. It is here that my books can assist. As a mother, grandmother, and great-grandmother, I know that all kids relate to animals, and the first ones they meet are their household pets. Then as they venture out, they meet Farm animals and learn new words like duck, pig, horses, and cows, and they soon discover the habits, sounds, and colors of their new friends. Then a visit to the Zoo introduces them to the world of Nature, and it is essential to teach them to respect without touching our natural environment.

I grew up on a farm and have lived on one most of my life, so it's a subject that comes easy. My coloring books are designed to teach kids to respect the world they live in.

They are published in collectible series with different coloring pages for different ages and interests.

If you like this book, please follow my other series, and if you would give me a good review as an author, I would greatly appreciate it.

This Book
Belongs to ME

Save the Bears

Coloring Book

Save the Bears

Coloring Book

Save the Planet Series

SAVE the BEES

ACTIVITY and COLOR

100 Page BOOK

Save the Planet Series

SAVE the BEES

ACTIVITY and COLOR
100 Page BOOK

Save the Planet Series

Save the Planet Series

SAVE the TURTLES
Activity and Color
Save the Planet Series

Jeri Lee C.Ht.

Save the Wolf

Coloring Book

Save the Planet Series
Jen Leechi

Connect the dots

Save the Planet Series

Save the Wolf

Coloring Book

Save the Planet Series

Jeri Lee C. Ht

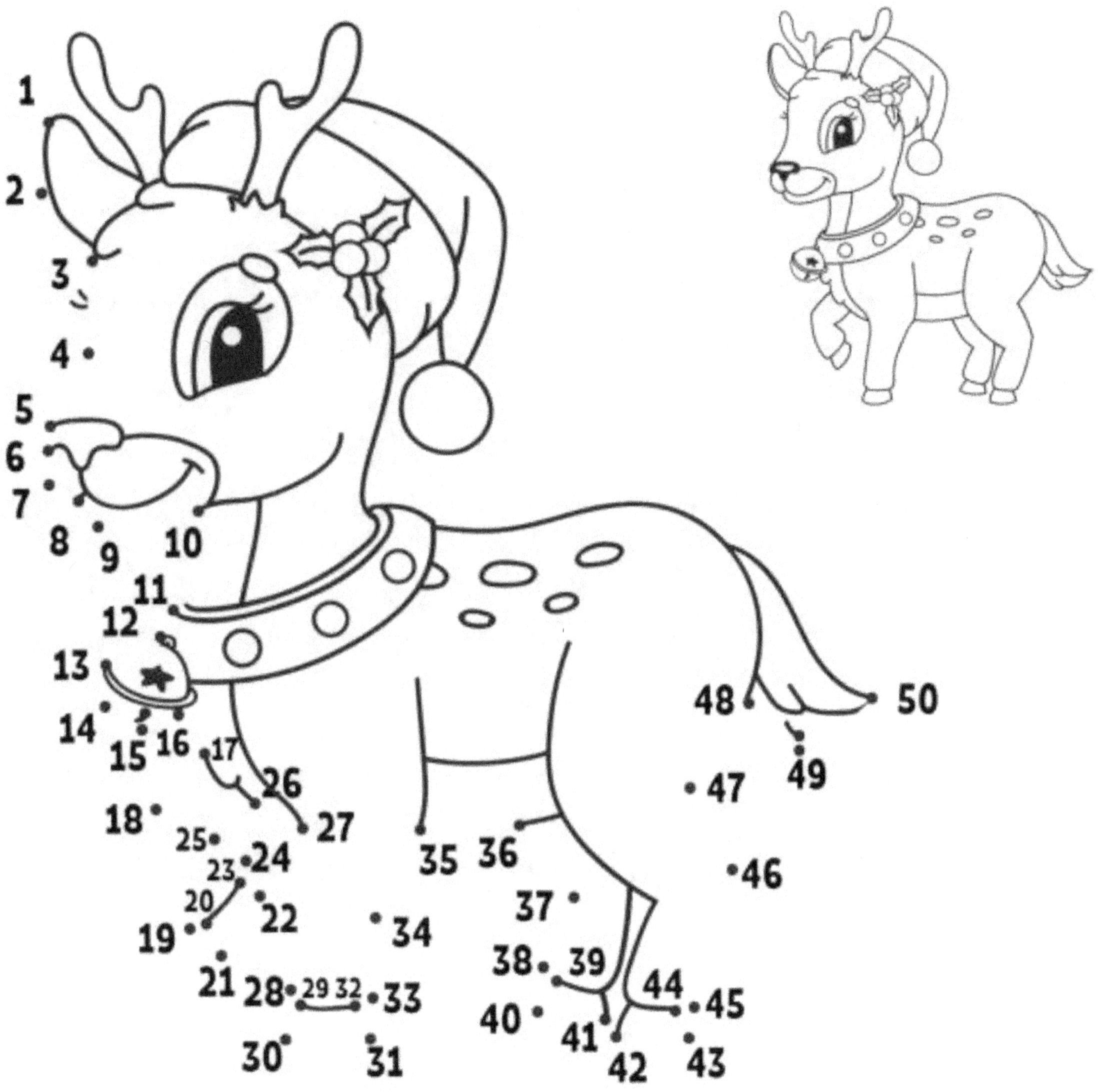

Save the Planet Series

COLOR
Butterflies

for

Adults and Teens

Save the Planet Series

COLOR Butterflies

for

Adults and Teens

ANSWER: 1. cup 2. plate 3. blanket 4. cake 5. deer

Save
the
BIG
CATS
Coloring Book
Jeri Lee C.Ht.

Save the Planet Series

Save the BIG CATS

Coloring Book

Jeri Lee C.Ht.

Connect the dots

Save the Planet Series

Activity and Color Book

Save the Planet Series

Save the Elephants

Jeri Lee C.Ht.

Save the Planet Series

Activity and Color Book

Save the Planet Series

Save the Elephants

Jeri Lee C.Ht.

HOW MANY?

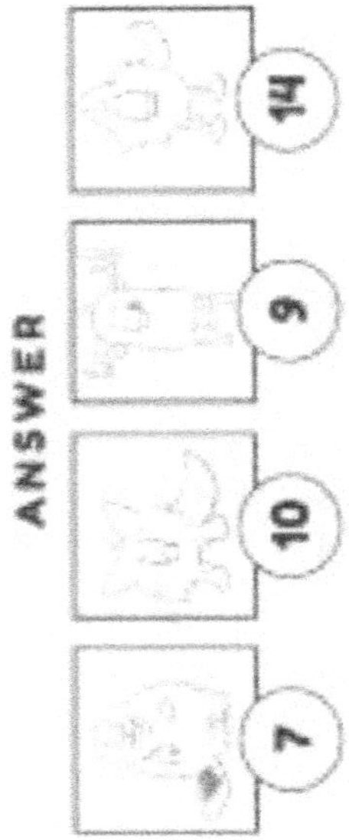

ANSWER

14

9

10

7

Save the Planet Series

OUR
PLANET

Activity and Color Book

Save the planet Series

Jeri Lee C.Ht.

OUR
PLANET

Activity and Color Book

Save the planet Series

Jeri Lee C.Ht.

Save the Planet Series

Coloring Book

SAVE the PLANET Series

Jeri Lee C.Ht.

Merry Christmas

Save the Planet Series

Coloring Book

SAVE the PLANET Series

Jeri Lee C.Ht.

Color

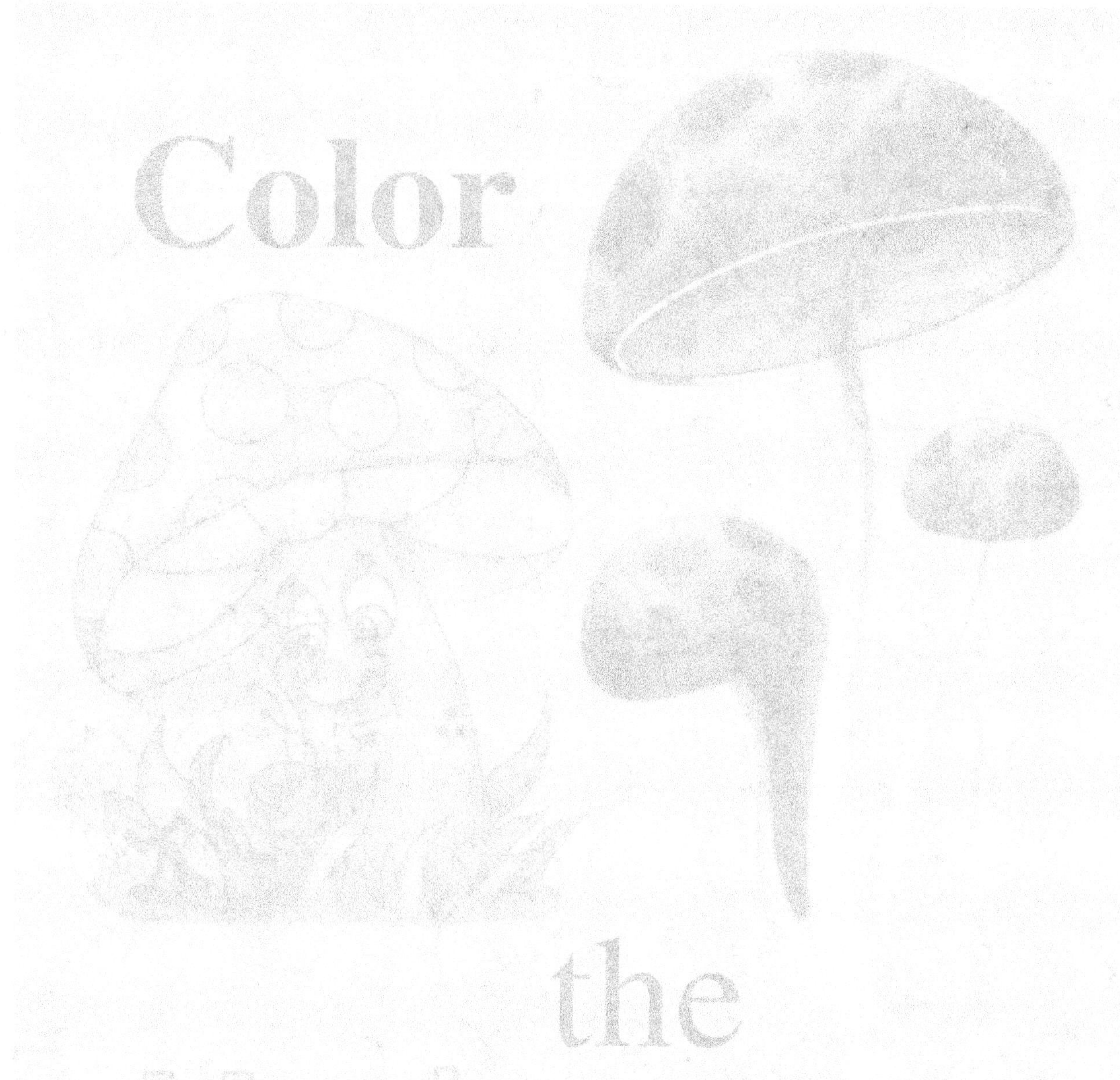

the

Mushrooms

Coloring Book

Save the Planet Series

Color the

Mushrooms
Coloring Book

Save the Planet Series

Save the Owl
Coloring Book

Save the Planet Series

Save the Owl
Coloring Book

Save the Planet Series

Save the Planet Series

Save
the
Giraffes

Coloring Book

CHRISTMAS
crossword puzzle
1.
2.
3.
4.
5.
6.
7.
8.
9.
10.
11.
12.
ANSWER
1.Elf 2.Snowman
3.Santa 4.Sledge
5.Gingerbread 6.Stocking
7.Mitten 8.Present 9.Sweater
10.Penguin 11.Tree 12.Deer

Save the Planet Series

Save
the
Giraffes

Coloring Book

Save the Planet Series

Save the Planet Series

Save the

Frogs

Coloring Book

For Adults and Teens

Save the Planet Series

Save the

Frogs

Coloring Book

For Adults and Teens

Save the Dolphins
Coloring Book

Save the Planet Series

Save the Planet Series

Save the Dolphins
Coloring Book

Save the Planet Series

Save the Fish
Coloring Book
Save the Planet Series

Save the Fish
Coloring Book
For Adults and Teens
Save the Planet Series

Save the Planet Series

Save the Whales

Coloring Book

Adults and Teens

Save the Planet Series

Save the Whales

Coloring Book

Adults and Teens

Save the Planet Series

Save the Planet Series

Save the

EARTH

Coloring Book

Jeri Lee C.Ht.

Save the Planet Series

Save the

EARTH

Coloring Book

Jeri Lee C.Ht.

Save the Planet Series

Flowers

Adult Coloring Book Series

Save the Planet Series

Save the Planet Series

Birds

Coloring Book

Jeri Lee C.Ht.

Save the Planet Series

Birds

Coloring Book

Jeri Lee C.Ht.

Family Pets Series

I Love My DOG

COLORING BOOK

Family Pet Series

Jeri Lee C.Ht.

Family Pets Series

I Love My DOG

COLORING BOOK

Jeri Lee C.Ht.

Family Pets Series

Dogs
Coloring Book

Floral Wing

ButterFly

Coloring Book

for All Ages

Save the Planet Series

Family Pets Series

Farm Animals

Match the

Jeri Lee C.Ht.

Family Pets Series

Color Cats

for Adults and Teens

Am I a Hampster Or a Guinea Pig

BOOK

HELP LITTLE DEER BRING THE FLOWER TO HIS MOM

Family Pets Series

Kittens
for
KIDS
Coloring Book
Family Pet Series

Family Pets Series

Rabbits

Coloring Book

Family Pet Series

Family Pets Series

Coloring book

FISH

1 - light blue   2 - blue   3 - green   4 - dark green
5 - yellow   6 - orange   7 - gray   8 - brown   9 - black

Family Pets Series

Coloring Book

Horses

Family PET Series

for All Ages

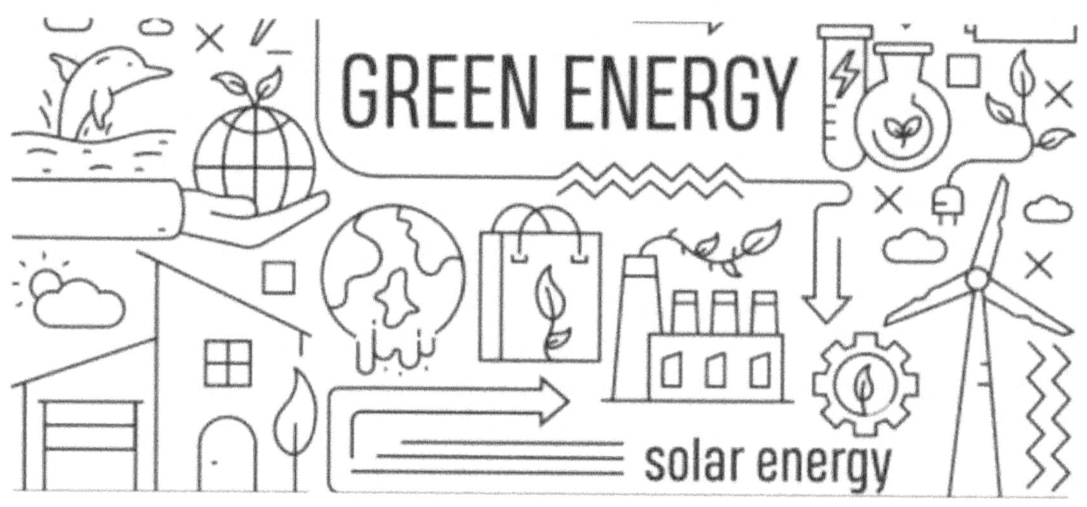

With respect for our planet and the disrespect of how its population has treated it either knowingly or unconsciously, I believe we all share the guilt of its destruction and the responsibility of its rescue. I share with you the echoing voices of two of its most recent authorities on the subject and pledge to do my part in helping the planet help itself.

Albert Einstein said: The world will not be destroyed by those who do evil, but by those who watch them without doing anything. Everything that exists in your life, does so because of two things: something you did or something you didn't do. Failure is success in progress.

Stephen Hawking said: Remember to look up at the stars and not down at your feet. Try to make sense of what you see and hold on to that childlike wonder about what makes the universe exist. It is very important for young people to keep their sense of wonder and keep asking why.

We are only the temporary custodians of the particles of which we are made. They will go on to lead a future existence in the enormous universe that made them.

With this series of books Save the Planet, I hope you share these values with me. I was born in 1939 and have watched the planet get small enough to fit into your living room while losing the true meaning of nature. So I am requesting your help in rectifying the damage.

t

save
OUR
PLANET
Activity and Color Book
Save the planet Series
Jeri Lee C.Ht.

SAVE
the
TURTLES
Activity and Color
Save the Planet Series
Jeri Lee C.Ht.

SAVE the BEES
Save the
BEES
ACTIVITY and COLOR
100 Page BOOK

Save
the
Bears
Coloring Book

Activity and Color
Book
Save the Planet Series
Save the Elephants
Jeri Lee C.Ht.

Color
the
Mushrooms
Coloring Book

Save the Whales
Coloring Book
Adults and Teens
Save the Planet Series

Save
the Wolf
Coloring Book
Save the Planet Series
Jeri Lee C.Ht.

SAVE THE
EAGLES
Coloring Book
SAVE the PLANET Series
Jeri Lee C.Ht.

Save BIG
the CATS
Coloring Book
Jeri Lee C.Ht.

COLOR
Butterflies
for
Adults and Teens

Save the Planet Series
Save
the
Giraffes
Coloring Book

Save the Owl
Coloring Book

Save the Fish
Coloring Book
For Adults and Teens
Save the Planet Series

Save the
Frogs
Coloring Book
For Adults and Teens

Save the Dolphins
Coloring Book
Save the Planet Series

UNIVERSAL

PEACE